The COMEBACK

The COME BACK

DARRIN WILLIAMS

COOKE HOUSE
PUBLISHING
WINSTON SALEM

THE COMEBACK
Copyright © 2016 – Darrin Williams

All rights reserved. This book is protected by the copyright laws of the United States of America. This book may not be copied or reprinted for commercial gain or profit. The use of quotations or occasional page copying for personal or group study is permitted and encouraged. Permission will be granted upon request.

Unless otherwise identified, Scripture quotations are from the King James Version. Copyright © 1982 by Thomas Nelson, Inc. Used by permission. All rights reserved.

Design by Cooke Consulting & Creations LLC
Cover Design: Tia W. Cooke

Soft cover ISBN: 978-0-9979923-2-8
eBook ISBN: 978-0-9979923-3-5

Library of Congress Cataloging-in-Publication Data
Names: Williams, Darrin
Title: The comeback: fighting back with faith / Darrin Williams; LCCN: 2016952709
LC record available at https://lccn.loc.gov/2016952709

Cooke House Publishing
(a division of Cooke Consulting & Creations, LLC)
Winston-Salem, NC
publishing@cookecc.org

This book and all Cooke House Publishing books are available at Christian bookstores and distributors worldwide.

Printed in the United States of America.- First Edition

DEDICATION

Today I have the opportunity to thank God for all he has done in my life. This book is the first of many. After 12 years of being saved, I finally have the release to publish my first book. God gets all the glory! Thank you Lord for leading and guiding me every step of the way. I will continue to give God the praise for the rest of my days.

    I thank God for all those who have supported my wife, Michelle, and I since our conversions. I thank you! Thank you to my mother Denise; my father Jeffrey "Jafar;" my sisters Natashia, Janzi, and Anitra; my brother Robert; and all of my nieces and nephews. Thank you to Michelle and I's grandmothers – both of our maternal grandmothers are named Betty – and to Roberta and Henrietta. Thank you to my uncle Antione and Aunt Kietra.

    Thank you to my mother-in-law Sheila, the Simmons family, the Kelly family, and the Raglin family.

    Thank you to our church family at New Beginnings Outreach International and to the Body of Christ that we have served with in ministry all these years. For every invitation to minister, we thank you.

    Last but not least, thank you to my Roo family. To my wife Michelle, I love you baby. My children Zeira, Zemry, and Quintesha. My grandchildren (my $1000 children "theROOkidz") Zaleyah, Zyirah, Zemry Jr. and Ze'Amber, Poppie loves you all.

                                    Blessings to all.

CONTENTS

PREFACE 9

CHAPTER 1
I REMEMBER 11

CHAPTER 2
FLOUR PARTY 15

CHAPTER 3
SLUGGER GROWING UP 19

CHAPTER 4
CHUCK E CHEESE'S 23

CHAPTER 5
MY HIGH SCHOOL YEAR 25

CHAPTER 6
DO WHAT I HAVE TO DO 27

CHAPTER 7
NEW BEGINNINGS 29

CHAPTER 8
CALLED TO THE WORK 33

CHAPTER 9
PLANTING A CHURCH 101 37

CONTENTS

CHAPTTER 10
PLANTING THE BIGGEST SEED   41

CHAPTER 11
KINGDOM ORDER   45

CHAPTER 12
WHY CHANGE?   49

CHAPTER 13
THE SOURCE   53

CHAPTER 14
COMEBACK   57

CHAPTER 15
COME OUT THE CAVE   61

CHAPTER 16
2ND ATTEMPTS   65

CHAPTER 17
WHAT'S NEXT?   69

CHAPTER 18
IDENTITY   73

CHAPTER 19
MY BOO, MY BABY, MY RIB   77

PREFACE

Finally, I can tell my side of the story! This day and age is based around the internet, the world wide web. That's great! It has been a great tool for business, educational purposes, and we can't forget social networking.

My approach with the internet is to communicate my passion for Jesus Christ and how He has changed my life since parting ways with the world's systems.

In this book I invite you into our world. I can't tell the entire story so this book will only be snapshots of our life, but it will give you a better picture of how God, the Creator of us all, orchestrated my life. The key is to embrace the Creator and live according to His will in your life. My wife, Michelle, and I encountered many hardships as youth. In many respects those hardships shaped us to depend on God wholeheartedly. As a result, as we stayed connected to the Vine, we yielded much fruit. So buckle you seatbelt; this will be a ride!

When you hear the words, "I didn't do it!" instantly you think the person saying it is not telling the truth or lying to get out of trouble. Just like when a parent comes in the kitchen and sees a glass of spilled milk, the child quickly responds, "I didn't do it!" Perhaps the glass just fell or someone accidentally knocked it over, but what essentially the child is telling their parent is that although they are present, they didn't do it.

The point of the above story is to let you know that "I didn't do it!" When it comes to how blessed my family and I are, please know that we didn't do it. We cannot take credit for any of it. So, the question is who did it? God did it! Our Creator! Brace yourself for the journey you're about to experience through our eyes. We give God all the glory!

Welcome to the snapshots of the Roo family. The COMEBACK!

Chapter 1

I REMEMBER

As far back as I can remember I always knew I was very special. I knew deep down inside that I was somebody. It took some time to find exactly who I was and what I was born to do, but thankfully I discovered it.

I was born in the heartland on the border of Missouri and Illinois in a town called Alton, Illinois. It all began in the summer of 1980. Summertime in Alton is full of fun, excitement, and babies! One afternoon on August 3rd, the proud 16 year old mother, Denise "Nise" gave birth to her baby boy. My grandmother Betty who I refer to as "Mama" said that my mother was banging on the walls so hard that she was going to call me "Slugger" because Denise was "Slugging them walls, saying 'Get it out of me.'"

I'm sure my father was happy because another baby boy came into the world. I am my father's third child out of five. My father's name is Jeffrey; he is also known as "Smitty Roo." From what I was told he was a smooth cat, handsome, and very ambitious. He traveled all over the country at a young age moving around to various cities trying to find his way in life. He only had an eighth grade education, but he was a quick learner and great with his hands. He could draw very well and was also a poet. With the rise of the disco party scene in the 70's, he worked at several clubs as a valet and security guard for many celebrities. Many say I look like my dad.

We moved several times growing up. The West Coast, particularly California, became my second home. My parents live there presently. At four years old I took my first trip from Alton to Los Angeles. That is almost a 1600 mile trip through farmlands, mountains, and the desert. It was so exciting. I ate all the snacks a kid could have. At each store we stopped at I grabbed up all the junk food I could – Zoo Zoo's, Wham Wham's, Oreo cookie, chocolate milk, Mike & Ike's and so much more. I paid for it though as I developed a horrible stomach ache. Travelling from state to state and seeing all the scenery was such a joy to me. We made that cross country trip in an AMC Gremlin. It is now known to be one of the 50 worst cars of all time, but back then it was great. It was small and compact, and since I was such a small child, it felt like a SUV to me. I was sliding all around in the back seat as my dad was speeding through the mountains.

Also, I'll never forget giving my dad kisses when I was still wearing diapers. I would hug him and kiss him but I didn't like his mustache because it was bushy and prickly. His mustache felt like a steel Brillo pad, but I looked forward to his hugs and kisses. My dad would be out hanging with friends and when he would come home I would rush him with excitement.

While we lived in the Dooley Projects, my dad would come and go. I could tell he was actively in the streets because I would be so happy to see him when he came in the house wearing his signature white sleeveless t-shirt. He would go to the closet and grab something, give me hugs and kisses, and then disappear again. My dad was a hustler.

I also remember riding my tricycle outside. I was told to stay on the sidewalk but since the other kids were riding down the hill I decided to try it out. I fell and flipped over so hard. I had scraps and scars and was bleeding. I think my mom recognized my cry and came to my rescue. After all that, you would think I would stay on the sidewalk, but a few months later, I was right back at it again trying to ride my bike down the hill.

I remember when my mom and dad's relationship ended. One day my dad came to visit me and our visit lasted longer than my mother would have liked. He took me to a field and we sat there as he talked to me. We were actually just in the woods sitting on the grass in the adjacent projects called Alton Acres; however, that day stirred up a lot drama as everyone thought my dad had tried to kidnap me. I think he wanted to spend some extra time with me as he knew their relationship was over and he probably wouldn't get to see me as often as usual. Later, my parents rekindled their relationship and soon it was time to go to California to get away from it all. Several years later my mother had a baby girl, then 11 months after that, she had another baby girl so now our little family grew to five. I was happy because I was glad to be a big brother and help my younger sisters.

Chapter 2
FLOUR PARTY

We began to move all over Southern California. We lived in 4 to 6 different cities; at times we lived in apartments, other times we lived in roach motels. We also lived in our car for a while. During this time things got darker for my parents. This is the first time I knew something was different but I believed it was masked with me being a good big brother. I had the pleasure of being on big brother duty more and more frequently watching my sisters while my parents would go to the store. I come to realize now that during this time my parents' addiction was maturing from just fun times into a monster of its own. So I would baby sit much more often.

Once I was watching my sisters. I believe I was in the second grade at this time because this was a season where I didn't attend school. As an aside, not being stable in one residence kept me from enrolling in the school district. In California they have a track system. The children would be placed on different tracks. To give you an example, Track A goes to school in July and Track B would start a month later. The tracks differed by the amount of kids and start dates. So with those different start dates plus no permanent residence, I missed a portion of the second grade. One night my sisters were playing like normal. I didn't think anything of it. They often became wild as most toddlers do, but there was something different about this day.

I was doing my routine check, making sure everything was intact in the motel room. I enter one room and I hear cries. My sister has a plastic spoon in her mouth and when she jumped off the table, the spoon hits the back of her throat. She begins screaming extremely loud. I also notice that she is covered in some type of white powder. I scan the room and it looks like an explosion at a flour mill. Everything in me is dreading the trouble I believe we are in. I try my best to calm down my screaming sister and wipe up as much of the flour as I could before my parents returned.
The flour was in their hair, their diapers, absolutely everywhere. It was too much for me to clean up all by myself. But we didn't get in trouble after all. As I look back at this situation as an adult, this really was the beginning sign that my parents had an addiction. The white powdery substance looked like flour, but really it could have been something much more dangerous.

Several people who lived at the motel had addictions. The motel was a haven for criminal activity. I saw a heroin addict convulsing from seizures right before my eyes. Her granddaughter would tell me she had to help her grandmother out when that happens. So it was almost second nature to have a family member on some kind of controlled substance.

That motel holds loads of memories. However, we moved around a lot. We were even in missions a few times. Like the L.A. mission also around Skid Row. Skid Row is a city inside of a city. Skid Row is known to be the place where the homeless and impoverished lived. We had to frequent these areas. The good thing about these places are they offered meals and shelter for those in transitional situations like we were at that time. From the projects to different hotels to apartments and even our car, we lived all over. Compton, Upland, Redlands, Rancho Cucamonga, Hollywood, Palmdale, South Central, Hawthorne, Gardena, Pasadena, and North Hollywood were all places I remember, but I'm sure there were more. Sometimes we lived with family and friends, but through it all we made it.

Later that year my parents separated again, so my mother, sisters, and I moved back to Illinois. Being that I missed so much school I had to repeat 2nd grade. I didn't know anything! It was hard to adjust in school since I rarely attended school. So I tried my best but it didn't seem good enough.

I affectionately refer to my mother as "mother dear." It is a term of endearment. Our relationship has been filled with many ups and downs. Calling her "mother dear" makes me feel warm inside. Well, time passes and mother dear gets a new job. So now we got our own place. We moved to the Joesting projects. Many called it "Joe stank" because there was a large sewer system on the edge of the project line. The smell was bad but we played in it anyway. The kids from "the Joe" would ride our bikes, fish, and even swim there. It was a lot of fun for us; you would've had to live there to understand. We lived in the Joe for few years.

Chapter 3
SLUGGER GROWING UP

At 12 years of age I wanted to be cool. So I decided to gangbang and joined a gang. At that time it seemed like the best thing to do. I went to school in a part of town where the Gangster Disciples (GD) ruled but most of my family was Vice Lords. So one day after school a group of GD's tried to jump my cousin. I was not going to let that happen. I had his back When the GD's saw that I was there to help him and even the odds, they backed off. From that day forward things changed.

I got baptized at the age of 10 while we lived in the Joesting projects. We were very active in church. I served as a junior deacon and usher. I would read my Bible often. But even so, it still was not enough to keep me from wanting to be in a gang. At 12 years old, I became a Vice Lord. Word quickly got around that I was in that gang. I would wear my hat to the left side of my head. I would have yellow and black rags. I would also throw up gang signs and did the Vice Lord handshake.

My life begins to shift again. My dad, who I haven't in 4 or 5 years, comes back to Illinois. I was happy to see him, but so much was different. He was smaller than I remember and had a West Coast accent. He had served time in jail and had been shot multiple times. Seeing him reminded me of the time we were living in California and he came home with his shirt in his mouth. The shirt was full of blood. Someone had broken my dad's jaw. He didn't tell us why but I believe it was because he was on someone else's turf getting money. They had to wire his jaw shut. I remember growing tired of him calling me through his shut jaw. I had to help him eat as he had to drink all of his food through a straw.

Now that mother dear and my dad are back together we move Uptown. Uptown was essentially Vice Lord territory. Being cool and part of the Vice Lord gang, I started carrying a shotgun in my pants leg. We lived with my dad's mom for less than a year. Then we moved to the Alton Acres projects which was Gangster Disciple's territory. We actually moved next door to rival gang members. They were older than me but my older gang members had beef with my neighbors so it would be tense at times not knowing if something bad would happen when they would come to visit or pick me up.

Having my dad back around was cool but I was grounded all the time. I had to talk to my girlfriend on the phone while my friends and their girlfriends were at the movie theater. My dad would make me draw and watch the Discovery Channel while I was on punishment. But eventually it wasn't so bad as he would allow my friends to come over even though I couldn't go anywhere with them. Everyone loved my dad. He was a jokester and would always have everyone laughing.

During the summer of 1995, I was going to football practice for Alton High School. I had a nice arm so I was going to try out for quarterback or running back. I finally made it to high school. The older guys would say, "Lil Slug made it to the Bird." Alton High was known as "the Bird" because the school mascot was a redbird.

But things came to a halt. My mom got hurt on the job and received a large check. I didn't know it would be both a blessing and a curse. The blessing was that we had money but the bad part was I only attended Alton High for six days. After football practice my parents said, "Go home and pack!" By the time I arrived home, the U-Haul was packed up and we were ready to go back to California.

We moved to Palmdale, California which is about 1 hour north of Los Angeles. My first day of school at Highland High (the Bulldogs) was like going on a college campus tour because the school was so big. The varsity football head coach took me under his wing that first day and I started learning pass plays and started lifting weights.

We moved again to another apartment that was on the bad part of town but closer to the Hammock Recreational Center. It was there that I became really good at basketball and gave up on football with the hopes of entering the NBA one day to get my family out of the ghetto.

Chapter 4
CHUCK E CHEESE'S

August 3, 1995 was my 15th birthday and it started as a great day in Sunny California. This day was filled with promises and anticipation. Even though it was my birthday, I wanted to do something special for my younger sisters. So my mom accepted my request to take my sisters to Chuck E Cheese's. The plan was to get ready then head to Gardena and enjoy "our" birthday. I told my sisters this is their day as well and me being the big brother was going to treat them to a great day of fun and pizza. At this time, we were living in a motel again, so it took a little time for everyone to get dressed and ready as we all share the one bedroom. After my mom and some of her friends got ready, they left saying they would be back in a few minutes and then we would all leave to enjoy my birthday.

My sisters and I are so excited, talking about how much fun we will have and what we will do once we arrive at Chuck E Cheese's. It is now about 3:00 pm. The suspense is growing. Time continues to pass and 5:30 pm rolls around. We are still believing that it's enough time for us to have fun at Chuck E Cheese's even though it's a 45 minute ride to get there. To let off some steam, my sisters and I go outside to play while we continue to wait for our mom. I am thinking that there's no way she forgot about my birthday. But now it's 9:00 pm. I don't even remember if we ate anything all day, but we are still waiting on our mom. My sisters are looking to me for an answer but I don't have one. Hollywood Boulevard is at its peak now as pimps, prostitutes, and dope dealers are starting to come out, so it's time for us to go back into the motel room. Exhausted from anticipation, the keys began to open the door. My mother comes in, her eyes are bloodshot red, and my heart sank.

My mother forgot me on my birthday. She had been out doing drugs all day and partying on my birthday without us. From that day, some of the love I had for my mom began to dissipate. I was so heart broken. I still loved my mother, but now it was different. I didn't want to be let down again, so I thought that if I didn't love her as much anyone, it wouldn't be that easy to break my heart next time. I held on to this pain for more than eight years.

Even now I treat others to Chuck E Cheese's on my birthday for this very reason to give others what I didn't receive – a chance to enjoy my 15th birthday. I finally forgave my mother when Jesus came into my life. I told her how I felt so I would have closure. What stuck out to me was grace. I had to give her grace because she was in her addiction and I know she would have did what she could if she was in her right mind, but I thank God she got her deliverance. Chuck E Cheese's was the beginning of her addiction being visible to me.

Chapter 5
MY HIGH SCHOOL YEAR

Being a new student at school was almost a norm. We moved so much but I really enjoyed it. It was almost like a movie where I could be someone different at each school. We loved watching movies and had aspirations of being in the film industry. My parents took us to many movie auditions and also modeling agencies. I received 7 stars when I auditioned for the movie "187." Hollywood Studios gave me great reviews. My parents were $2,500 short for my shot of being a model with Barbizon modeling. My family did not have money to fund my acting and modeling career, so I still believed that the NBA was going to be my way out of the hood.

But life is tough. My mom is now working at a prison but she and my dad are still using drugs. I remember on my 16th birthday, he gave me $300, but a few hours later he asked for it back. He used the money to get high. To keep myself focused, I played basketball. It was a way for me to keep my mind off of all the bad things that were happening in my life.

My parents' drug addiction was at an all-time high. My parents separated again and my sisters and I moved in with my mom's friend as we couldn't go to a shelter because they didn't allow males. So in 1998, I packed up and flew back to Illinois. My uncle Antoine "Boo" was my life saver and role model. I could always count on him.

Those goals of making it in the NBA never left, but my dream came to an end. I was back at Alton High school but because of my grades, I couldn't play, and this was my senior year. I could practice with the team but I couldn't play even though my skill level was higher than the starters on the team.

Eventually I did get an opportunity to play. I knew that if I didn't do something to wow the crowd and coach each time I was on the court, I wouldn't get noticed. So for the few minutes I was allowed to play, I made sure I did something that would make the highlight reel. My coach wasn't happy because I would not run the plays he wanted, but I would amaze everyone and score each time I had the ball!

I got accepted to Robert Morris College in Chicago, Illinois. I worked as a valet at a local casino all summer. I saved every check; however, I made so little that it only added up to enough money for one month of rent. I was going to try to walk on the basketball team. But it didn't work. Things got worse because after the season at Alton High, I began to smoke weed. Prior to this I always said no to drugs and would talk about athletes who did drugs. But I fell right into the trap; smoking weed became how I eased my mind. My dream of being in the NBA and providing for my family is officially over.

Chapter 6
DO WHAT I HAVE TO DO

The summer after high school graduation I knew I had to make a choice. I moved in with my father's mother and got into a "do what I got to do" mode. I began to hustle. Since there was no NBA contract or movie deal, I had to find a way to take care of my mother and sisters. I was always a good kid, but by 19 years old I had seen and experienced so much, I ended up making a wrong choice. I became a drug dealer and was addicted to the fast life of making money. I would hustle for days at a time wearing the same clothes. I became addicted to grinding because I was addicted to the money. But after the money, cars, and rims, there was still a void – a hole in my soul. I was lost and didn't know where to turn. My flesh loved it. My spirit was getting tired of broken relationships and going to jail. From 18 to 23 years old, my life was in disarray. I was arrested multiple times, in gang wars, and even got car jacked. I was shot at 4 times, with 3 times happening the same night. Because of decisions I had made, I was facing 6 to 15 years in prison because of cases stemming from gun, mob action, and weed charges. In 11 months, I was facing charges for three different cases.

I remember I had bought a 1982 Pontiac Bonneville. I had it painted white and blue pearl. When the sun hit it just right, you could see the blue pearl shine. I also paid $3,000 for some 18 inch rims, had installed a new stereo system, and had a Chevy Corvette engine with shift kit. You couldn't tell me I wasn't cool. But this didn't last long. One day, my best friend, my cousin, and I were in my car and I hear the words, "Don't none of ya'll move" from the voice of a guy I don't recognize nor have I ever seen before. We didn't move! This guy starts shooting and a bullet hits the driver's side door. I crawled my way through from the driver's to the passenger's seat and out of the car. We had been drinking and smoking all day, but I sobered up immediately. My car was gone but I was alive!

    I remember being at my dad's mother's house and watching TV. Whenever I would come inside from hustling, the TV would always be on the Christian channel TBN. I would watch and then go back outside and keep hustling. Even during the times I was in jail, I told the Lord that if He got me out I would live for Him. He got me out but I would go right back to hustling when money ran out. However, I knew I couldn't keep playing with God. Being named Slugger, I knew that three strikes means you're out. I was already on my second strike.

    Life is rough and with all the trouble I'm in, I had to move with my Mama, my maternal grandmother. I was on intense probation where I had to be at home by 7:00 pm every night for 15 months. By the time that probation was over I was rapping in a local secular rap group. By May of 2003, I stopped slanging for good. I gave it all up. I paid off all of my street debts and starting working at a warehouse. With all I had been through, I was super stressed and had lost 30 pounds. Working at the warehouse helped me to get myself together. I was still drinking and smoking but I had turned a new leaf. I was a legitimate working man trying to change.

Chapter 7
NEW BEGINNINGS

In June 2003 things start looking up for me. I am finally getting myself together. I am feeling good about myself. I started being active in sports again and I feel like I am somebody. Many ladies at the warehouse seemed to be interested in me. However, there was one young lady who sparked my attention. She was my friend's cousin. My friend and I worked in the back of the warehouse unloading the trucks to stay out the way so we could go smoke weed outside. I approached her but she didn't pay me any attention. When I asked for her number she said that she was too old for me. I found out she was 11 years older than me. But I didn't care because to me she only looked 20 years old. She was beautiful, well put together, and wore her own real hair! One day she approached me to talk to me because she said I was looking sad. This was the opportunity I needed and I went for it.

She was in a relationship but he was in jail. Her car was also giving her problems, so I took this as my chance to step in and help her. I would take her to work, the laundromat, and to church. She was also getting her life together as she had a rough upbringing. Her name was Michelle nicknamed Cook short for Cookie. We referred to her as Cookie but now she goes by Lady Roo.

At the age of 5 years old her father was killed. Her mother became addicted to heroin and was an abuser for 18 years. So Lady Roo and her brother lived with their grandmother. Her grandmother took care of 9 kids. Her grandmother raised her six biological kids plus three of her grandkids. Lady Roo's mother was serving a 3-year prison sentence and would send letters from prison. Lady Roo was a hustler as well. She hustled for years until her children got older. She didn't want them to get caught up in that lifestyle. Lady Roo was touched by her mother's letters and began to make changes in her own life, which included attending church more.

I would take her to church then go smoke weed. We began to get closer. Around Thanksgiving of 2003, I made the decision to stop smoking and drinking. I went to the club the last time during this time. People would say things like, "Slug, it looks like you are wearing a church outfit."

I was pretty fresh but I did look like I was going to church. I knew then that things were about to change. Lady Roo's mother was released from prison. When I met her all she talked about was the goodness of the Lord. I remember God but this time I was listening. I had been through so much in just my 23 years on this earth. I had to get back in tune with God. A few weeks went by and each day I could hear voices in my head saying, "You're going die today. You're going to go to jail today." So I knew things had to change. And boy did it change! I turned my back on the street life. I turned in my player card. I stopped going to clubs and I turned my entire life around.

December 14, 2003 is the day I became born again. Normally, when it was time for church I would drop Lady Roo off then go smoke, but this night I told her I was going to go with her. She thought I was lying but this time instead of dropping her off I went inside with her. The service was good. I was wearing a gold chain, my hair was in a ponytail and my gold teeth were shining. I was a straight thug in church. I hadn't smoked or drank for two weeks so I was sober and knew what I was doing. My future mother-in-law said, "Slug you need to get saved." The service was already over so everyone was leaving, but she said it again. I turned around and a prophetess began to give me a word. The word was from God because I did not know any of those people. I asked the Lord into my heart at the front of the church. I repented for my sins and asked the Lord into my heart. During the years prior from getting in trouble with the law I was talking to the Lord but this was my time to give Him my whole life. Slugger Roo Got Saved! The crowd rejoiced by praising God. Then the Bishop asked me did I have anything to say.

I said "No" but my hand grabbed the mic and I said, "I am going to keep my braids and gold teeth and rap for Jesus!" I give the mic back and everyone was just looking at me, then they started to praise God. As we left I was just in deep thought. We arrived home and I just started to read the Bible. Lady Roo's children asked me "What's wrong, Slug? Why are you so quiet?" They were so used to me always rapping and being high. It was apparent that something was different. I told them I am saved now and I need to know what this Word says. To date, I have read the Bible three times completely.

Also that night I wrote my first gospel rap. It was titled *Lord Jesus Christ*. I had my first performance at the same church in January 2004 at a Martin Luther King, Jr. event. It was awesome. The mayor and other officials were there and the church was filled to capacity. As only I could, I brought my own flavor to it. I had someone make a hockey jersey in the church colors with "Slugger Roo" and #1 on it. I didn't take my jacket off until after it was my time to rap. I gave my testimony and then took my jacket off. The crowd went crazy!

That was the beginning of the Slugger Roo era. From that day I began to rap for Jesus for real. That year alone I rapped 52 times and also had my first national television appearance. Just starting out I didn't have any beats, so I rapped with a clap or instrumental. The word spread like wild fire. I was an ex gangbanger/drug dealer now rapping for Jesus. The editors of newspapers became interested in my story. I was featured in all the area newspapers, a Christian magazine, as well as on television.

...

#*Rooflexions:* How to get a fresh start.

Most think you just need to erase and start over. That's where we miss the whole process. In life you can't just erase your life's experiences like they never happened; you have to embrace what happened. When you embrace what happened you can find the joy in knowing there is a purpose for everything you have been through. Then you are able to have a truth moment with yourself where you lay everything on the table – the good, bad, and the ugly. After you see the outcome of the hard times, you make adjustments. It's similar to mathematics. You add God and all the good things, and subtract the bad things that will hinder your fellowship with Christ.

#*Roocouragement:* Start fresh where you are!

Today is your New Beginning! Don't let yesterday's pain or shame hold you back from your fresh start. The amazing part is we become new with Jesus. We think with a new mind which gives us a new talk then a new walk. You become a new person then comes new opportunities. New doors will open for your life. It will be hard work but the things you care about you fight for. Fight the good fight of faith for your new beginning! It is worth the fight; don't give up just yet! Today is a new day.

The Comeback

Chapter 8
CALLED TO THE WORK

We are now dedicated to the work of the gospel. I've been rapping for a couple of years at this point. We feed the hungry, witness on the streets about Jesus, and feel the burn to preach all the more. We began serving our pastor as armor bearer then the call to preach came in July 2005. I preached my first message called "Going Through" on October 23, 2005. One thing about Lady Roo and I is that we persevered. We never gave up!

I am excited about our COMEBACK! The last 12 years from 2003-2015 have been swift and trying. I gained such an anointing though! I thank God for the anointing; it was not cheap or easy!

Here is a snapshot of our timeline after being born again.

2003   Met Lady Roo in June. Accepted Christ in December.
2004   Married Lady Roo August 1; First National TV appearance as a gospel artist; Rapped 52 times without any financial assistance; Quit working at the warehouse so I could complete community service

••• 33 •••

to finish paying off probation fees. At the time, I owed more than $3,000 for court and probation fees. My job didn't pay enough to pay those fees in a timely fashion. So I quit the job at the warehouse to do community service every day to pay off those debts.

2005   Marriage back on track as we got in agreement with each other and with God; Started new job at American Steel Foundries (ASF) in April and each year our income increased substantially I was hired at ASF in April of 2005; Probation ended in May of 2005; Moved into townhouse four months after starting job at ASF.

2006   Formed Slugger Roo LLC - that is our independent entertainment company with many divisions from media (film/music) to photography and clothing.

2006   Released first album off our independent label "Slugger Roo Entertainment."

2008   Recorded first music video; Lady Roo laid off

2009   Released 2nd album *R.A.P.* - *"Revelation And Prophesy"* Laid off in March from ASF

Life changing time! Here is where we begin to place all our trust in God!

2009   May started "The R.A.P. Tour" in May while both of us are receiving unemployment; July Started Barber College

2010   April Graduated from Barber College; July Facing eviction; Opened our first barbershop in October

2011   January released 3rd album *The Union*;Moved into new home in October with only $400 in savings; Took a hiatus from music to focus on family and ministry; in November Lady Roo starts 2 new jobs.

2012   April stopped accepting unemployment insurance. God told me that He would sustain me. I also accepted the call to Pastor and in June

	launched a church inside of a barbershop.
2013	June moved our church services to a hotel; In October made the decision to use our personal savings of $8,000 that was initially going to be used to buy our first home plus $3,000 of church savings to purchase church facility and new barbershop.
2014	In June, God released me to start my music ministry again; Celebrated my second year as pastor; in November we only have $16.00 but both our church and home bills are paid in full each month.
2015	The foundation is laid and now is the time to build! We made sure that we put our trust in Jesus alone for everything. Our foundation is in the Word of God. So now through faith in the Word of God we can continue to build in all areas, from our home life to the ministry, all at the same time.

Through it all we never gave up! This time we are working smarter, not harder. Thank God for the anointing and the leading of the Holy Spirit!

In 2012, God told me that He would sustain us and that He is our source. And we believed Him. This is just a glimpse of what we have endured. Also during this time, we lost a host of loved ones to murder and incarceration, but we still pressed. In fact, in 2015 between the two of us, we lost 7 family members. I had to eulogize one and that was tough, but there is definitely a blessing in pressing. The burden we have for souls is like fuel for the fire. To see someone's life transformed or to finally get a breakthrough gives us great joy. We know our reward and our prize. If the Lord can do it for us then He can do it for anyone!

...

#*Rooflexions:* Working for the Lord is all about balance.
From home life to marriage to family. You can't have one without the other. Having a spouse who has the

same vision is key. Agreement will be the deciding factor on the success of the work. If the home is not right, anything outside the home will not be right. As LadyRoo and I finally came into agreement about what to do next, the vision and dreams we had began to unfold in our favor. We decided to make the Lord Jesus Christ our top priority. Once we made that decision, our life became a reflection of our connection to Christ. Being connected to God has transformed our life and the way we live our life sends praise to God because we are working for Him. Just like working a job and receiving their benefits, there are many benefits to working for the Lord. Favor is one of them. The favor we have experienced in our life just by trusting God is unexplainable. Move by faith. Try it again. You have tried many things. Try Jesus this time. With Him as the foundation, all things will work together for your good.

Chapter 9

PLANTING A CHURCH 101

First things first—you must be called! That is what many have said. I know this to be true also. Planting a new ministry is not anything that someone should do on their own. The task is so great. It will take God's grace to bring you through what He sends you to. I hope you caught that. Like Abraham, God spoke to him and said, "GO." Truthfully, that is all you need to send you on your way. Like the Bible says, "Send me, I will go!"

After you accept the call, you will probably have many questions as to how it all will work out. From my observations, I have learned that when you are connected to a denomination, some things will be in place to help the launch. Even a launch team will help aid the launch. All that is great but that is not my story. Like Abraham, Michelle and I just had a word from the Lord. I give God all the glory for allowing us to find our way in ministry from the ground up.

We simply had a burden for the lost. Because of how the Lord completely transformed our lives, we wanted to share Jesus with the world. Pastoring takes this burden to a new, higher level. Prior to pastoring, Michelle and I served three different ministries and worked closely with them. I believe it shaped and molded us into the leaders we are today. We have seen the blessings and the struggles, the good and the bad, and what works better than other things or ideas.

We first began holding prayer services in February 2012 in my barbershop. I rented a space from New Beginnings Salon. I coined my side of the salon "New Beginnings with Roo Barbershop." I am also a barber so the idea was to use the barbershop like a substation for the ministry we were part of, but God had a bigger plan. Our prayer meetings led to "Break 'N Bread" Bible studies. Our Bible study has an open forum style where all can interact, share their thoughts and opinions, as well as ask questions. It has been very successful for us. In the beginning our numbers were small so we met bi-weekly. At our very first prayer meeting, someone sowed $200 into the ministry. We also had eight in attendance. That was enough confirmation for us as the number eight represents new beginnings.

In May of the same year our pastors released us to do the work of the ministry, just like Jesus gave His disciples power and sent them two by two to do the work of the Gospel. May was our sending moment. That was when it began to really set in. It is time to go forth with this call; there could be no turning back now. In June we held our first Sunday service in the barbershop. It could only hold 25 people comfortably but that didn't stop us. Normally I would work every Saturday from 10:00 am until 7:00 pm, often times without any breaks, and then rearrange the barbershop to ensure it was set for Sunday service.

This was a very humbling experience that taught us both how to appreciate the small things. We held service in that location for one year. We saved every offering we received totaling $3,000. By 2013 we had outgrown the barbershop and needed more room for our growing congregation. The services for our first year anniversary and pastoral installation were held in a hotel. So I asked the hotel staff about renting out the ballroom on Sundays. By the end of June we had signed the contract to begin holding weekly services at the hotel. At this time, the church membership had grown to 100 members.

Even though we were now worshiping in a hotel, we already had a location in mind—a 5,000 square foot facility that we desired. We contacted the owners and maintained contact with them monthly. There was an issue with the roof that was going to cost $125,000 to repair. We didn't know how, but we placed that matter in the Lord's Hands. After only 16 months of ministry, the door opened for us to lease the facility.

Michelle and I have learned from many before us that the Heavens are opened. God is just waiting on us to release in the atmosphere what it is that we need. So we always pray hard during July 27-August 5th. Those dates represent our own personal holy week. We choose that time every year to pray, fast, and seek God's will for our life and the ministry. By August 5th we were contacted by the owners of the buildings stating that they had the funds to repair the roof! Praise God!

...

#*Rooflexions:* A prayer for the planters

I pray in the name of Jesus for those who are in leadership to be movers and shakers for the Lord. Be strong, courageous, and full of faith. I pray for strategies to expand the Kingdom of God through you. I pray for favor over your life in Jesus' Name!

Be diligent! Write your plans down. Write the vision then walk it out. When you plant a seed in the ground you are expecting it to grow. Keep your expectation high! Use everything around you that you can use. Don't focus on what you don't have, but use what you do! You have more than you think. We do not profess to have all the answers, only the Lord does and we just do what He instructs us to do. Follow Him. Be like Abraham: listen then proceed in faith.

Chapter 10

PLANTING THE BIGGEST SEED

This next season was crucial for the future of our ministry and my business. At the advice of the hotel manager, we had entered into a month to month contract, so that we would not be locked down in the event that we found a building. We knew that this was God because the owners of the plaza where the facility is located are ready to move forward with letting us lease the building. At the same time, Michelle and I are preparing to purchase our first home. Prior to beginning to pastor, we moved closer to Alton, IL to be closer to our business and the church we attended. In a couple of years, we had saved up $8,000 and cleaned up our credit to become homeowners.

We are now praying for the funds needed to move forward with leasing the building. Not only do we need the down payment and deposit, money is needed for renovations as well. The building we had in mind was not ready but the two buildings next to it were. So the owners wanted to meet to show us the two locations. This was perfect for the phase we were in ministry. Two buildings with 4,000 sq. ft. combined including office spaces.

We told the owners our vision as well as letting them know that we needed to run the barbershop out of the same space. They agreed. During my prayer time I heard, "Get

My house first. You have the money." I rebuked those voices because I believed surely that was the devil speaking. But Michelle and I both prayed and talked about it and agreed that we should focus on the Lord's house first.

So we used the $8,000 we had saved plus the church's $3,000 totaling $11,000 to secure our new location in Alton Plaza. We did not let anyone know what we were doing. After signing the lease, we had a short 16 days to get everything in order as we gave notice to the hotel that September would be our last month holding services there.

Ironically, as soon as we signed the lease for the church, our home landlords asked were we going to purchase our home. We told them exactly what the Lord told us about getting His house first. They understood and said we could just renew our lease. What an amazing God!

We surprised our church the last Sunday in September letting them know that day was our last day at the hotel because the next Sunday we would be in our new location. They were speechless. We were known as a barbershop having church; now we are a church with a barbershop! We also have our film and recording studio in our new building. They each have their own space, but at this time, the Lord told us to go on another hiatus from rapping and also our new film/photography company to focus on building the church.

So we made the best decision to sow into the vision first with our faith seed. We put all our money in. Some would say we went broke but we say we sowed a seed and are expecting a great harvest.

...

#Rooflexions: What is Your Seed Worth?

To walk in this type of faith you must understand the power of the seed. We have seen God send overflow into our life from giving financially to others, churches, and charities. Sowing and reaping is a principle to live by. You give, you receive, and you give again. It would have been easy—and some would say it would have been right—to buy our home first. However, we choose to look at life differently. Our thought became what about the souls that would be saved through our church. A soul is more important than any material possession.

Nothing that is planted grows overnight so you must look at the future. Your seed may birth youth recreational activities and other things that will help your community and build the next generation of leaders. Many times you will have to move past what will bring you the most pleasure and consider the bigger picture. We are proof that if you take care of God's House, He will take care of yours.

Chapter 11
KINGDOM ORDER

The number 12 is often said to be the number of governmental order. The number of 12 is considered a perfect number and symbolizes God's power and authority. There are 12 tribes of Israel; 12 gates in the New Jerusalem; and even in our judicial system, 12 serve on the jury. So 12 is a very strong number. As of 2015, we have been in ministry for 12 years. I said before that 2015 will not be like 2014. We declared that we wouldn't be broke another day in our life. After sowing our personal savings, Michelle's car broke down in December 2013. A few days later, she purchased a car with no money down. We talked to the salesman while I was at work and by that evening we drove home with a new car!

At the beginning of 2014, the church had $0 and we had $0 but the church expenses and our personal expenses added up to $5,000. Our faith was stretched to a whole new measure. The Lord made a way out of no way. We had grown as a church but still didn't have the adequate amount of finances to pay our yearly expenses of $25,000. Our church, New Beginnings Outreach International, grew to 100 members and we did a great job with the small team we had. We were few in number but mighty in God.

That made our faith stretch again seeing how God made a way for us as we continued to forge ahead. Money was never our goal. Our goal was to preach Jesus, but as we began to take territory, "seed" was needed to plant in new ground in order to do what the Lord had called us to do. We are a firm believer that you cannot make an appeal for money, asking others to sow if we didn't do it ourselves. So we showed and taught the congregation how to sow.

I was not focused on that mainly. I was focused on how God was still opening doors for the ministry in spite of the lack of seed money. What we lacked in money, we made up in faith. Our 2014 slogan was "No lack, no luck, but all faith." It was truly that. As a young pastor facing many things I always stood in expectation of what God was going to do next.

Whenever someone of the Kingdom of God carries the anointing, God's presence will follow. Since we have been in the plaza, the plaza has been upgraded with a new roof, new parking lot, new awnings, and new buildings built on the land. It was similar to Obed-edom's experience in 2 Samuel 6:11-12:

> And the ark of the Lord continued in the house of Obed-edom the Gittite three months: and the Lord blessed Obed-edom, and all his household. 12. And it was told king David saying, The Lord hat blessed the house of Obed-edom, and all that pertaineth unto him, because of the ark of God. So David went and brought up the ark of God from the house of Obed-edom into the city of David with gladness.

I told the owners about that passage of scripture and they replied, "God is with us."

...

#***Rooflexions:*** Order!

With things in the right place, things will come to order. The first is that you must build your foundation in Christ, and walk by faith and not by sight. Trust Him. The Lord will provide, even when the facts on paper say that there is no reason for it to work out. I have learned not to focus on the paper nor the numbers. Secondly, we must remember we are *servants* of the Most High God, so everything we do is for His glory. We are the hands and feet of Jesus called to work the Kingdom of God. So get your things in order. Pray, plan, and then proceed!

Chapter 12
WHY CHANGE?

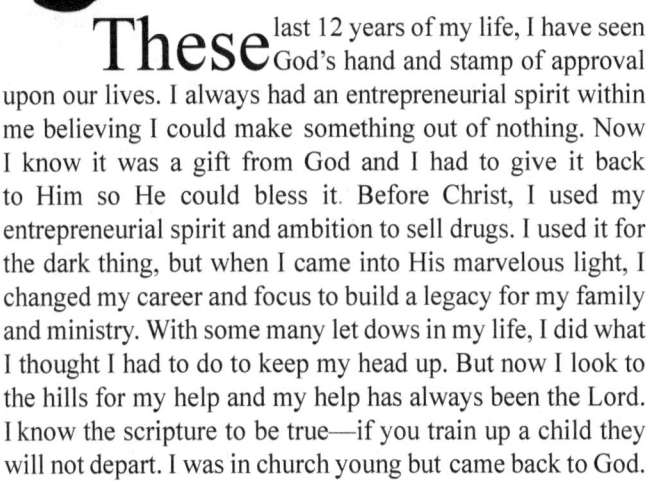

These last 12 years of my life, I have seen God's hand and stamp of approval upon our lives. I always had an entrepreneurial spirit within me believing I could make something out of nothing. Now I know it was a gift from God and I had to give it back to Him so He could bless it. Before Christ, I used my entrepreneurial spirit and ambition to sell drugs. I used it for the dark thing, but when I came into His marvelous light, I changed my career and focus to build a legacy for my family and ministry. With some many let dows in my life, I did what I thought I had to do to keep my head up. But now I look to the hills for my help and my help has always been the Lord. I know the scripture to be true—if you train up a child they will not depart. I was in church young but came back to God.

From all the things we have experienced we have learned how to make something out of nothing. We knew that the systems of this world can fail anytime like they did when the economy turned in 2008 which made it hard for families. So we decided to invest in ourselves. In 2006 we invested to get Slugger Roo LLC off the ground. We got that name trademarked and registered. The first part of this enterprise is music. We have released 3 albums and a few singles from our own record label to date.

We knew we had something special. Our music ministry began to grow a following from basically being real. Our testimony really was needed to help others know that Christ is the way. Our plan was to always strive for excellence with professional CD duplication, HD music videos, and quality sound. From there our company began to move into film and photography.

Because of a love for video production back in early 2000's when I was still in the streets, I had an old video camera that used VHS tapes. I would film our life on the block. We made several recordings and called them "Tree Life" because the place where we hung out was called the Tree. This sparked my interest even more, so in 2010 we invested in a better camera. Now we could produce our own videos! In 2008, we were the first Christian Rap artists in the St. Louis area to have a HD music video who weren't signed to a major label. I really developed a passion for videography then. I saw what the director did and believe I could do the same thing. Plus that would free up a lot of funds so that we could continue to grow as a company.

Our first album, we paid for studio time, photography, and professional duplication. Moving forward, we invested in all areas from video to recording. One of my younger cousins sowed a seed into our life which I used to purchase our own home studio. We have been pouring our own finances in our company since 2009 and everything since that time has been produced and filmed in-house. We produced 2 more albums plus several high quality music videos. Our videos aired on many major Christian TV networks like TBN's JCTV. All of this is happening and we are an independent record label. The Lord has been gracious to us and has opened many doors for Slugger Roo LLC.

Our company has also produced work for other artists, preachers, and businesses. We took a hiatus from all of that in 2012 to plant a church. So we just stopped right in the middle of growing a power house company. However it was worth it as God used that time to infuse us with new revelation. So when we moved into our new facilities there was enough space for our recording studio and film/photography studio to function as an in-house company but also available for others needing professional services.

So the change from street life yielded great results that lead us to trust God first then invest and watch God open the doors. This is our testimony that God has done everything and He gets all the glory. Once we gave our life to God He became our source, so when jobs and others failed, the Lord held us and kept us flourishing.

...

#Rooflexions: Change is necessary!

In life there are steps we have to make in order to facilitate change. Think about when you are driving and come upon a road where there is heavy construction or the road is not complete. If you continue down the road, you'll probably end up with serious damage to your vehicle and possibly yourself and any passengers that are with you. Instead, you must change directions, make a U-turn, and go a different route. Life is about finding a better way. We must find a better way to get to where we feel in our heart is God's plan for our life. Knowing that you are doing God's will be a blessing to you even if you have to change and it takes longer than you anticipated. Life is a journey and there is nothing wrong with doing things over or trying another way to get the best outcome. Don't be afraid to change courses. Make the change and begin moving in the right direction.

Chapter 13
THE SOURCE

Make the Lord your SOURCE! Once we made the Lord our SOURCE, our life has never been the same. I trusted the Lord because He blessed us with increase. Before I was laid off from the steel mill in 2009, I was making $60,000 a year. When that ended, it made life even clearer. I knew that I needed to trust in the source more than the blessing. The blessing was the job but the SOURCE gives you the job/provision.

Also don't allow your blessing to turn into a curse. That happens when you trust in the blessing more than the SOURCE. I was led to go into full time ministry before the layoff but I stayed longer than I was supposed to and ended up being laid off. I was more concerned about my check than just walking in faith. But situations will happen in your life that will make you go directly to the SOURCE.

As soon as I got laid off I took about 3 months off to clear my mind and rest. I hadn't seen my mother in 4 years, so she was my frist business to take care of. I flew to California to see my family. When I returned from California, I was focusing on touring with a tour called "The R.A.P. Tour" that began May 2009. It did well but I knew that it could kill us before it could bless us financially. We didn't receive much from booked events and when you add in promotion of the tour on a national level, there just wasn't enough funds coming in for that to be our sole source of income.

During this time all our funds from Slugger Roo LLC were depleted because there wasn't much additional income. As part of our layoff deal, the steel mill offered to pay for any school if we chose to attend school. I went to the unemployment office to set that up and to the trade readjustment facility. I was looking for something to further my career in music production. They didn't have anything in that field. So after prayer I thought about barbering. I have been barbering since I was 12 years old. At first I was told that there weren't any barbering programs either. But one was found. And not only was it paid for, but they also paid for my transportation. Our SOURCE was providing.

I could have went back to the steel mill. They even called me but I did not return their call because I knew what the Lord was saying to me and I did not want to be disobedient again. So I stayed in school. I still toured and did ministry while in school. When I graduated from barbering school, I knew I would have my own shop. The SOURCE opened a door. My cousin's mother-in-law had a salon called "New Beginnings Salon." It had a barbershop on the other side that had not been used in several years.

I graduated in April 2010 but didn't get the shop until October of that same year. Michelle and I remodeled the shop to our style and began to build our clientele. The plan was to get people "fresh for less" to make a name for ourselves. It worked but it was tough. I remember there were days when I would only make $7 a day. There were even days I had to make it home on an empty tank of gas in my SUV.

The time working at the barbershop wasn't even like a job. Because the barbershop had been closed for more than three years, we had to revive it. Many days we would arrive at 9:00 am and not leave until 10:00 pm, and even then we wouldn't make $20. We didn't have any flyers so we made signs by hand and I would stand outside and dance around while holding a sign that read, "Barber on duty. Fresh Cuts." It was truly a humbling experience. Imagine a man and woman who had been on many media outlets around the nation now holding a sign for cheap haircuts dancing on the corner in the hood just to survive.

But in April 2012 the Lord spoke to me and said, "I will sustain you!" I knew then He was my "SOURCE." At the time, our unemployment benefits were paying all our bills. My wife was laid off about 6 months before me. So her bills became my bills. The bills were paid but there was never any overage. We pressed on anyway. Michelle didn't get another job until November 2011. She was unemployed for almost 3 years. During that time, we worked at the barbershop together.

So after hearing the Lord say He will sustain me, I knew what I needed to do. I had to cut all ties to anything not coming from God, which included unemployment. On top of the Lord telling me that, I received a letter from unemployment stating that in order to receive any more money I needed to make a "sustained work search." The word sustained was in bold black letters. That was my confirmation to open my own bank account for myself and become fully self-employed.

Once I did that the income from the barbershop almost doubled to what we were receiving in unemployment benefits. I then prayed for more effectiveness. God gave me the idea to raise my prices by $3 and to move to appointments only. That was one of the best decisions I ever made and was the beginning of seeing the Lord as my "SOURCE." From 2012 we have seen a lot of abundance in our life all by the leading of the Lord.

...

#Rooflexions: He really is your source.

When making God your only SOURCE you put yourself in complete submission. You don't worry about what it looks or feels like, you just submit to Him. Doing this may seem like one of the most challenging times in your life, but I promise if you submit to Him and the process, it will also be the most rewarding. God will give you strategy and it will produce. Watch as you make the Lord your SOURCE, you will see how He enlarges everything according to His will for your life. Stay connected to Him. It's easy to take your eyes off of Him and begin to move in your own strength and trust other things to provide. And for a while it may seem like it is working. But I promise if you seek God as your source and provision, you will grow by leaps and bounds, and your own house and ministry will be blessed beyond anything you can imagine.

Chapter 14
COMEBACK

Before you can have a comeback you must first have endured some setbacks. It was truly a divine calling to walk out this task of believing God's word. All we had was trusting the Word the Lord gave us. If the Lord told us to go, then we would go and wait until the Lord said where. The Holy Spirit has truly been our guide, our teacher, and our comforter. There were many moments where we thought we would barely make it, but the Holy Spirit would give us another Word of promise.

In 2014 I declared that 2015 would not be like 2014. We declared that we would not lack or be broke another day in our lives. But after sowing all we had plus ensuring the church bills were paid, we were depleted. From October 2013 through November 2014, our finances were bleak. But we still had the Word of God that kept us optimistic. I told everyone I was already in 2016 and we hadn't even entered 2015, but I was a year ahead in the Spirit.

At the lowest point during "our drought" the Lord showed me "the abundance of rain." One day I looked out the window at the barbershop and it was raining pretty hard. I was on the phone with my wife and said, "Baby, I need to go get my jacket. It's raining outside." She was in another city about 25 miles away and told me that it wasn't raining where she was. I finished closing the shop and as I stepped outside, I was amazed at what I saw. It was no longer raining, but there were rain drops *only* on my car. I rode by other cars to see if they were wet, and to my amazement, they were all dry as if it had never rained. I logged onto a social media site soon after and saw a well-known preacher post that she can hear the abundance of rain. That was my confirmation. I held onto that word. The abundance of rain is here!

As 2014 ended we received yet another confirmation that we had to experience the comeback first so those following us can see it is real. Even before 2015 my wife and I received a seed on the same day from two different people totaling $150.

Now the church is not in a good state financially. In fact, the church's bank account was negative. Even so, I would often tell my wife that the church is doing better than us. We did not let it get us down because we knew we sowed and a harvest would come in due season. We continued on like we always have—preaching the gospel full in power and unwavering. We are broke financially but rich in faith.

I am big on the meaning of numbers and seasons. Being a Seer Prophet those things speak to me. To make a long story short, after almost 2 years of struggling financially, we got everything we sowed back! On the first day of Spring 2015, the church had its money back plus we did too. It was a sign of the comeback. We were in Chicago at a conference with many well-known preachers. The confirmation was just amazing because they were preaching on the same topics that I had preached about in the recent past.

So 40 months after NBOI was launched, we had our first revival. We called it the "Comeback Revival" and we had sessions called the "Comeback Revival Injections." The injections sessions' aim was to infuse the Word of God by injections on prayer, marriage enrichment, financial focus, and SOURCE and blessing. It was awesome! Lives have been changed since that conference. We are out of the drought because the abundance of rain is here! We are in the comeback!

...

#*Rooflexions*: A comeback.

     A comeback can be a number of things; it does not just refer to financial blessings. Joel 2:25 states, *"And I will restore to you the years that the locust hath eaten, the cankerworm, and the caterpiller, and the palmerworm, my great army which I sent among you."* If you continue reading, it is declared that the Lord will restore all you have lost. This Rooflexion is simple; don't lose hope. If you have lost anything, rest assured that a comeback is in your future

Chapter 15
COME OUT THE CAVE

The cave was a place we had to endure during a 5-year period. I thought it was just the time when I began to pastor but the Lord let me know it was 5 years. It began in 2010. The Lord told me to put everything on hold. He said to just cut hair and pastor. So all our other businesses that could bring in income had to stop. I believe this is where we learned patience and the will of God in the realm of trust.

We did not lean on our own understanding. Even when we thought about other ways to make income from our businesses, the Lord reminded us who we are in Him. I knew I could do nothing without the Lord. When I got saved for real I knew that in order for me to live on this earth I would have to yield my all to Him. By doing that I have seen His hand on our lives.

He restored the years! He restored the tears! He restored everything then He released us! Praise God! That is worthy of a praise break. Hallelujah! To finally be released to do what you have been in training for is great. The release to flow not just in your your local church but abroad. While we were in the cave, we had to be still. But we are grateful for the release to travel and minister locally and abroad.

We don't do this to see our names in flashing lights or to build big platforms, but to share the revelations and testimonies to the masses to encourage believers and unbelievers alike that there is hope through Jesus Christ. The cave has taught us about depending on God. We become God-dependent. Depending on God prepares you for the long haul without reserve. We believed and only moved when God instructed us to.

I will be lying if I say that coming out the cave is easy. After shutting everything down for five years, it can be a little daunting when you begin again. Just think of someone who has been in prison and is released. They are apprehensive and always on guard. We have been watching on the wall. Now it's time to do what we have to do for the Lord. The sunlight is bright for the prisoner who was just released. It takes some time to get used to it again. As such, the Son's light is different and others will know when you have been exposed to the Son's light.

Things we have learned while in our cave:

☐ Trust God with all our heart.

☐ God is our SOURCE.

☐ The Lord will restore the time and money.

Those three things will keep you in the midst of your darkest hour in the cave. Everyone's cave experience will be different. It all depends on what the Lord is trying to do with that individual. I believe that the cave is needed to purge and prune some things so that when you do arrive, you will know that it is the Lord that brought you out and got you to your blessed place. For some the cave is like a holding place or cage. It can also be a place to cover o shield you. Whatever your cave is to you, once you are released be prepared to soar like an eagle!

...

#*Rooflexions:* Cave Experiences

Cave experiences will differ but what is constant is that you are in one place for a period of time. Wherever you may be at this moment in your life continue to keep your gaze on the Most High. You were made to create and leave an impact in the earth. Learn the lessons you need to so that when you emerge from the cave there will not be anything holding you back from soaring. Come out of the cage and pursue everything God has told you to do!

Chapter 16
2ND ATTEMPTS

In 2015 the Lord said work smarter not harder. We aren't novices at being entrepreneurs. There are ups and downs, but if you work smarter you can stay level and afloat. With the Lord calling us back to the marketplace it is both exciting and refreshing. The great thing is we learned many lessons from our experiences. We planned before but after our cave experience, we found out more about ourselves and we learned how to be strategic. See, you can have a good idea but if you outside of God's timing, it won't work.

Our new facilities have space for all of our businesses. The rebuilding of the brand will be a snap this time. We have met many people along the way and are still in great standing with them all. This is why integrity and character is so vital to everything you do because either going up or down you will see the same person twice.

When someone builds a skyscraper they dig deep in the ground to lay the foundation. In the same manner, we have to be so rooted in Jesus that nothing will be able to shake us or knock us down. You have to be unmovable and unshakeable at all times, even when you don't want to be.

That is where endurance comes in. You must endure until your change comes.

Endurance is the key. In Galatians 6:9 it essentially states that your process of pain yields a great harvest if you don't give up. So what are you waiting for? Get ready to receive your harvest! You haven't gone through all you have to give up now! It's not time to sit on your gift! It's not time to wait! Get moving. Start that business. Plant that ministry. Restore that marriage. Walk into your season. This is your second attempt. Try again. Nothing is wrong with trying. The only thing that is wrong is when you don't try.

Pick up your bed and walk. Don't just lie there; get up! Begin to walk. Just take a step towards your victory. The foundation is laid, which is Jesus. It is time to build on that solid foundation so when storms come and winds blow it will not destroy that which has been built on that solid rock. So dust yourself off and get in the game. You're next up to bat! Put your dukes up! Time to get it in! This time you will do what needs to be done. The blessing of it all is you get another chance!

That is my outlook on a lot of things since being born again. See, the words have so much meaning to me to be born again. That right there speaks volumes that there is another attempt at life. Better life! Life with Christ is the best life. So now you are not doing things just for you but for the Father. Let His will be done. You get another chance but you're doing the Father's will which makes it easy because your aim is to please him. As you add the Father's will in your attempts you receive all you are focusing on. In His will He will provide all the things you need. He brings provision for the vision. Each business we started has been Christ centered. The focus was Christ so others will see Christ as we presented the business to the masses in the marketplace.

Experience has enlightened me that if Christ is the center of anything it will draw many. John 12:32 says *"And I, when I am lifted up from the earth, will draw all men unto myself."* Use your businesses as a witnessing opportunity to speak about our Lord. So not only introduce the products and services you offer but also introduce Christ. Use your business as ice breakers to expand the Kingdom of God. Each person you meet once you share the gospel they will share what you told them about the gospel with someone else. Seeds are sown with our words that falls on the hearts of men and the Lord adds the increase. So do I think Christ should be in our businesses? Of course! We are to be bold believers and unashamed of the gospel.

Someone may not go to church but they patronize your business which is gospel centered, so then you minister to them and they come to you for help. I have had many who would come ask for prayer. The real reaches the real! Your walk will show people if you are really about what you say you are.

That is your opportunity to serve. We are servants. We must be willing to wait on those who have requests. As we minister, we see how God has placed us at the right place and at the right time. Your light will shine its brightest when you are in proper alignment with your calling and are flowing in what God called you to be and do. It is not that hard to find your purpose. First start by thinking what is it that you like to do and what you are passionate about. Once you are clear on this, you are well on your way to operating in your purpose. When you determine your purpose, be the absolute best at it. Then present Christ in a way that others may see your greatness but know that there is one greater. This is your time for that second attempt. Get to it!

...

#*Rooflexions:* It's your time!

It's time to dust yourself off and try again. Try, try again, and keep trying. Remember, Fortune 500 companies did not quit the first time time; they kept going until they succeeded. The time is now; this is our opportunity to give it another shot.

Chapter 17
WHAT'S NEXT?

What is next for the Williams Family? I believe we are ready for lift off. We are locked and loaded. The seasons we went through were just practice. The Lord spoke to my spirit and said every year before 2016 was just practice. What an encouragement! He also said "I can't get better but you can." The Lord is perfect but we aren't, so we have opportunities to get better. Practice makes you better. You work on your strengths and your weaknesses at the same time you so that you will be ready for the game. Put me in, Coach!

You never practice to be MVP. You practice to get ready for the game. It's game time. Work smarter not harder was one of the goals for 2015 so I will do that from here on out. Planning strategic moves will place us in strategic places. From our experience, as you take care of the Father's will He will be working out what you are worried about. We had the Father's will on our hearts so much we forgot about our problems. Being locked into the vision we didn't get a chance to take our eyes off the prize because we have been on a mission. The mission had to be completed in order to fulfill that burden. Once we complete an assignment it gives us great pleasure to know that we were obedient to the call. We executed on time. Then we receive the next task at hand.

It doesn't stop for there is a great work to do. Each great work comes with a great prize. Pleasing our Father in heaven. John 4:34 says, *"Jesus saith unto them, My meat is to do the will of him that sent me, and to finish his work."* I truly believe that is what has kept us going. We are being fed. We never lacked. We were always on top as we did the Father's will. I think it is important to make a point here that even though life was challenging and we had a lot of hardships along the way, the truth is that we still were on top. In life, as long as you have clothes on your back and food to eat, all the other material possessions really do not even matter. We went through periods in life where there was nothing available. But we kept a childlike mentality—believing God knowing that He would take care of us. As children of God, He did just that; He clothed and fed us. We let God handle the rest as our Father. Our father took care of us during these times.

So we get to work our garden again. We already know what is in our garden. Our garden consists of all the talents we have that we cultivated into successful businesses. My love for cutting hair was planted at 12 years old and grew into a barbershop. The talent of rapping that was planted grew into a music ministry with an independent record label and studio. My love for film and photography grew into a photography studio. So as we work all we have in our garden it will continue to grow and yield much fruit in its season. We also know what it takes to produce a great harvest so this is another chapter in our lives where we can wait on the Lord in expectation.

Being late in the hour with Christ's return upon us, it is vital we use what we have. Use our talents. In the parable of the talents, the one who was a good steward over what they had gained more talents. We will not try to save anything. We will reproduce more. Pouring into others' lives has been in our hearts. This book is a seed to be sown in the hearts of many to know that we can overcome anything with

Jesus Christ once we allow His will to override our own. We truly can find our way in the world down the purpose highway. Situations happen on purpose for purpose. Your life is not just to have fun but to make your light shine for God. But have fun doing it. When you enjoy what you do it's not hard.

Proclaiming the name of Jesus is all we know. As we continue to lift His name He will draw others unto Himself. To see someone's life change for the better because you didn't keep all the goodness to yourself is amazing. You shared the Gospel. So we will continue to S.L.U.G.G.E.R.R.O.O.—"Spread Love, Under God's Grace, Everywhere, Respectfully, to Rejoice On & On." We are spreading the gospel through books, music, the barber industry, videography/film, photography, and ultimately, the preached Word. Those are a few things in our garden. You never know, the Lord may add to our garden in the next season. Whatever He does we are willing and ready.

...

#Rooflexions: What is in your garden?

What talents do you have? Be the best you that you can be. Being you can also bless you financially. My garden is full of things I enjoy and I get paid to do things I enjoy. I had to work my garden when jobs let me go. I had to go to my garden and work it until it produced a harvest. So you should do the same thing. Use what you have; use your talents.

Chapter 18
IDENTITY

Finding yourself is the best way to find God. You find out who and what you are from being unique with abilities that only you can do. Then you can be successful in all you do. Faith it out! You can make it out. Replace the "make" with "faith." You can faith it out! Having faith in God to bring you out as you find out who you are. Faith it to faith it! Your faith in God continues to grow as you are more comfortable in being the child of God you are called to be. Through your ups and downs you adjust your grip to hold on. Faith it until you make it! Your true identity is being a child of God.

    Once I realized that I am royalty, I put away the stigmas and statistics that would try to hold me down. When I read the Word of God, my spirit is strengthened. My spirit began to mature then the gifts began to be evident that my life had its own imprint. The place I was born, my parents, and my experiences all shaped my identity. The trials the tribulations, even my appearance made sense now. My braids and gold teeth will even be used as I am able to connect with others who look like me. It is all bait! It can be used to bring in others that can identify with something familiar. Being yourself will draw many.

I know that I am different to others but I am also the same to all. I didn't change my outer appearance to fit in. I stayed the same on the outside but my heart for God change on the inside. In the Kingdom we are made to be different for a reason. We are many members of the same body. Christ is the head but someone has to be the pinky toe. I love to say I will be the pinky toe, just let me wiggle. I do not care where I am placed. I am willing to work as part of the Body. So as you learn who you are you can function and walk out your purpose.

I had to find this out the hard way which was not a bad thing. I tried to fit in but I was so different. God lives inside of me but I look different from others. The words of 1 Samuel 16:7 became true to me. The Lord looks at the heart. People look at your appearance. It was hard in the beginning because I didn't know who I was, but I knew I was somebody. Then it was like a small voice saying, "Be who I made you to be." And so I began to embrace who I am—my braids, my gold teeth, all of me is who God has for a time such as this. With that being said, I had to step up to the plate and get ready to bat.

I knew if God was for me that was all I needed. That is also all you need. If God be for you great things can be done according to the will of God for your life. Embrace who you are in Christ. This is the key. I know that the braids and gold teeth can't hold me back. I know when and if the Lord tells me to change that about myself I will. I had waves before and I can wear them well. Until then I have to complete this assignment and reach those He places in my path.

Understanding the different seasons is key to identity. I go by different names depending upon the arena. From the gospel rapper to the barber to the pastor to husband to CEO. Each lane you are in you have to be authentically you. It will make things run smoothly because you are not faking it. When you try to be something you are not it will fall apart. So you must work on you. Work on character, integrity, and kingship. Your character will carry you a long way. Integrity is hard to find but many will respect you more if you have it. Kingship is your position in the Kingdom of God. You are royalty; joint heirs with Christ. That is your identity. You are somebody. You are valuable. Do you think the Father would have sent His Son to redeem us if He did not deem us worthy?

He loves us all with all of our differences that make us unique, but we all share the same opportunity to be saved from sin. Even though we have to be true to ourselves we have to admit we need Jesus to be whole. I found out that as I became washed in the Blood of Jesus in my mind, I really didn't care what people thought about me. As long as I pleased the Father and He knew me I was fine. My encouragement to myself is not to be who I used to be. I always strive to walk in the new me. The battle with the old identity is present everyday but that flesh has to die daily. My encouragement to you is to be holy, be authentic, and be you because now is the time to the find your true identity in Christ.

...

#*Rooflexions:* Be you and do you in Christ!

God doesn't want any carbon copies of the same person. He desires that we are honest with ourselves knowing we are nothing without Him. But He also wants us to be our authentic, original self. So don't worry about your appearance. God wants to use you just as you are. Be a new creature in Christ displaying the image of God to those around you. When they see you they see Christ. Shine for Christ in all you do.

Chapter 19
MY BOO, MY BABY, MY RIB

She is all I ever wanted. Beautiful, loving, and a go getter. Something like me but softer and smells better. Michelle has been the glue that has helped me be the man of God I am today. We had to learn each other. She made a decision to follow Christ and get baptized. Then a year later we met. Since I met her I knew I had to have her but I was looking for a wife. I was so tired of games and wanted to have one woman.

Her encouragement has been very instrumental to my growth as a man. Our first year of marriage was hard, but it helped birth our marriage ministry. We endured many things that gave us a heart for other married couples, letting them know that they can make it. We even made a song on one of our albums titled "The Union." The song was called "For All" on "The Union" album. That album was focused on married life. We know what it takes to make this marriage thing work. It takes God first, then the willingness to be humble and compromise to come into agreement. Agreement was key to overcoming the spirit of divorce. At one point, divorce was an option, but we held on and walked in agreement. The verse Amos 3:3 which says, *Can two walk together, except they be agreed?*" became real in our life.

In Feb 2005 we started to walk in agreement and our lives changed for the better. At that time, life was rough. I was on probation and it was hard to find a job. Many of our dates were at the probation office. I even had to quit my job at a warehouse to do community service to pay off $3,000 worth of fines. Even that was a blessing because I was being a witness to those I did community service with. So Michelle and I prayed like never before. We came into agreement.

Michelle has my heart because I have God's heart. When I submitted to God she saw the change and that made it easier for her to follow my lead without doubting. I always say I would marry her again and that is true. She is an awesome woman of God. She is small in stature but big in the Spirit. I call her my little pit bull because she is so rough but so lovely at the same time, and will not let go of God. Marriage is great especially when God is the center.

Our marriage life taught us that all the components have to work hand in hand to be successful. She is my boo, my baby, my wife, and my best friend. I enjoy being her husband, provider, and protector.

Here are a few pointers:

☐ Trust God

☐ Submit to God

☐ Keep your marriage holy

Once you have these down, then you can talk about finances, communication, and intimacy. God has to be first. This book is not about us but about God. We almost divorced but God! From my life I believe that thousands can relate to the fact that God is the SOURCE of it all.

The Comeback

When we realize that He gets all the glory. We can rest assured we have nothing to worry about because we are covered; covered by the Blood of Jesus. It is only the beginning for us. We are close to celebrating 13 years being saved and just celebrated 12 years of marriage. Use us Lord for your Glory! The COMEBACK IS NOW!

ABOUT THE AUTHOR

A native of Alton, IL, Darrin Williams faithfully attended church in his formative years but as a teenager he got off track and turned to the streets. From drugs to being a gangbanger to prison stints, his life was spiraling out of control. However, everything changed in December 2003 when he gave his life to God. His transformation came with a heart for the lost. He shared his testimony on several media outlets, including television, radio, and print publications. He has traveled across the nation as a Christian rap artist and it has opened many doors for him to minister on outlets such as TBN and JCTV.

In 2012, his burden for lost souls lead to the launching of New Beginnings Outreach International (NBOI). NBOI started inside of a barbershop but soon outgrew that space and now call home a 4,000 square foot facility in Alton.

Pastor Darrin is married to Michelle "Lady Roo," the love of his life. She aids him in family, business, and ministry. As leaders they use their gifts to share Jesus to all they encounter.

Since surrendering his life to Christ, he has seen the Hand of God move in every area. This is just the the tip of the iceberg, as Pastor Darrin knows that as he continues to seek the Lord, nothing is impossible.

To contact the author for speaking engagements, conferences, book tours and signings, write

Visit www.fightwithmyfaith.com
E-mail: dwilliams@sluggerroo.com

Other Authors by
COOKE PUBLISHING HOUSE

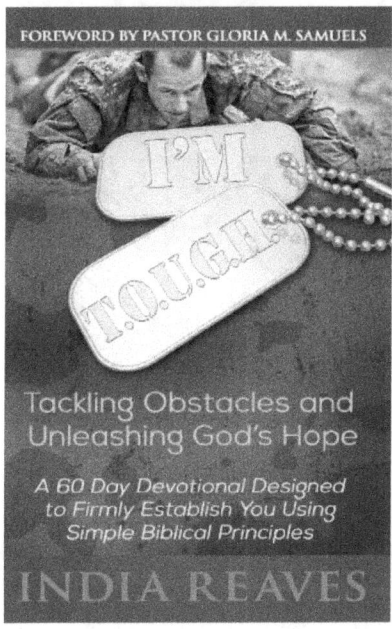

I'm T.O.U.G.H is a 60 day devotional book intended to resolutely ground the reader in a strong spiritual foundation. The messages in this book thrust the reader to think and reflect on their own lives and situations and to dig deep in themselves and be contingent on the victor that is in each and every one of us. Through scriptures, stories, personal testimonies, and teachings, readers will grasp hold to the fact that they are built to last.

ISBN: 978-0-6922-0263-0

For more information, visit
www.imtoughdevotional.com

Other Authors by
COOKE PUBLISHING HOUSE

Devastated But Not Destroyed is a divine interruption for those who may be headed towards destruction. It will jolt your faith, sustain your strength, and change your perspective from one of pity and pain to that of power. Discover how to master the moments of your life, pack up the pity party for good, and embrace the challenge of change. Everyone at some point will experience devastation, and this book serves as the go-to guide to rediscover the tenacity and fortitude necessary to avoid the pitfalls of destruction.

ISBN: 978-0-692-34201-5

For more information, visit
www.devastatedbutnotdestroyed.com

Other Authors by
COOKE PUBLISHING HOUSE

We speak of spiritual warfare in the same mindset as physical warfare. We have approached it with thoughts of violent and vehement confrontations. In actuality, spiritual warfare is best fought using simple biblical principles. 100 out of 100 people are offended, the offender, or both. This book is intended to teach one of the most basic, yet most powerful principles - and that is the principle of forgiveness. As you begin to practice this principle, you will experience a freedom in your spirit that you have longed to have.

ISBN: 978-0-692-30523-2

For more information, e-mail
scvinson@gmail.com

www.ingramcontent.com/pod-product-compliance
Lightning Source LLC
Chambersburg PA
CBHW070549300426
44113CB00011B/1836